RACE AND AMERICAN LAW

CITIZENSHIP, RACE, and the LAW

BY DUCHESS HARRIS, JD, PhD
WITH KATE CONLEY

Essential Library
An Imprint of Abdo Publishing | abdobooks.com

ABDOBOOKS.COM

Published by Abdo Publishing, a division of ABDO, PO Box 398166, Minneapolis, Minnesota 55439.

Printed in the United States of America, North Mankato, Minnesota.
092019
012020

THIS BOOK CONTAINS RECYCLED MATERIALS

Interior Photos: Shutterstock Images, 5, 30–31; Ah Xiong/Shutterstock Images, 8; iStockphoto, 11, 15; J.D. Pooley/Getty Images News/Getty Images, 16; Andrew Lichtenstein/Contributor/Corbis News/Getty Images, 18; Everett Historical/Shutterstock Images, 20, 42, 58, 64; J. Scott Applewhite/AP Images, 24; Hulton Archive/Archive Photos/Getty Images, 27; Underwood Archives/Archive Photos/Getty Images, 28; Pictures from History/Newscom, 34; Everett Collection/SuperStock, 39; Alpha Stock/Alamy, 45; Everett Collection Historical/Alamy, 51; Hulton Archive/Getty Images, 53; Paul Wagner/AP Images, 60; Bettmann/Getty Images, 63; AP Images, 68–69; Science History Images/Alamy, 71; John Preito/Denver Post/Getty Images, 75; Gene Blythe/AP Images, 78; Mark Lennihan/AP Images, 82; Pat Benic/UPI/Newscom, 87; Susan Walsh/AP Images, 88; Carolyn Kaster/AP Images, 92; Motortion/iStockphoto, 97; Steven Senne/AP Images, 98

Editor: Alyssa Krekelberg
Series Designer: Becky Daum

LIBRARY OF CONGRESS CONTROL NUMBER: 2019942073
PUBLISHER'S CATALOGING-IN-PUBLICATION DATA

Names: Harris, Duchess, author. | Conley, Kate, author.
Title: Citizenship, race, and the law / by Duchess Harris and Kate Conley
Description: Minneapolis, Minnesota : Abdo Publishing, 2020 | Series: Race and American law | Includes online resources and index.
Identifiers: ISBN 9781532190247 (lib. bdg.) | ISBN 9781532176098 (ebook)
Subjects: LCSH: Race relations--Juvenile literature. | Race discrimination in justice administration--Juvenile literature. | Conflict of laws--Citizenship--Juvenile literature. | Citizenship--United States--Examinations, questions, etc--Juvenile literature.
Classification: DDC 305.89--dc23

CONTENTS

CHAPTER ONE

THE DREAM OF CITIZENSHIP

Maria Praeli was living in Peru when her sister, Lorella, was in a devastating car accident and lost her right leg. The girls' father started transporting Lorella between Peru and Orlando, Florida, where she was receiving medical treatment at Shriners Hospital. The constant travel strained the family. They decided to get visas in order to legally live in the United States, and they moved to the United States in 1999. The Praeli family settled in New Milford, Connecticut, near family members.

"I remember arriving to America stepping out of the plane into the cold air and seeing my breath for the first time. I thought it was the coolest thing ever," recalled Praeli, who was only five years old at the time. "I remember my first days of kindergarten,

Immigrants to the United States come from all over the world.

how when I went outside for recess the playground was amazing. Nothing compared to the one—or lack of one—back at home. Ever since the moment I fell in love with the playground I have loved the public schools I have attended."[1]

However, that love grew more complicated over the years. The family members overstayed their visas. This meant they were living in the United States without the government's permission. They were undocumented immigrants. "When you're five years old, you don't really understand what's going on much less what immigration policy is like," said Praeli. As she grew older, the reality of being an undocumented immigrant became clearer. "I always knew that things were different," said Praeli. "My mom would always tense up when a police officer would drive by, and I knew things were harder for us, but I didn't really understand what being undocumented would mean for me."[2]

Undocumented Immigrants

Legal immigrants have permission to be in the United States. They can visit, work, and seek medical care. Immigrants who don't have permission are referred to as *undocumented* or *illegal aliens*. However, the term *illegal alien* has a negative connotation and dehumanizes people. Undocumented immigrants have either entered the country without permission from the US government or have overstayed their visas. If law enforcement officers learn of their status, these immigrants face deportation, which is the forced removal of a person for violating immigration laws.

AN UNCERTAIN FUTURE

Praeli wasn't alone in her struggles. Between 2012 and 2017, approximately 800,000 children arrived in the United States without permission from the US government.[3] The children have grown up in the United States, but because of their lack of official status, they don't have access to many of the privileges that legal citizens do. For example, they can't obtain a Social Security number. This number is required for getting a job and applying for government services, such as financial aid for college or a driver's license.

In an attempt to resolve this problem, President Barack Obama issued an executive order in 2012. It created a program called Deferred Action for Childhood Arrivals (DACA). It granted people like Praeli the opportunity to receive permission to stay in the country and work legally. The people who qualify are called Dreamers. However, DACA wasn't a permanent solution for Dreamers. In 2017, President Donald Trump let the program expire. As a result, Praeli and thousands like her faced an uncertain future. "I yearn for the day that I can live at peace and be on a pathway to citizenship," said Praeli in a 2017 interview. She went on to say, "I've grown up in this country, pledged allegiance to our flag since kindergarten, gone to school, and built a life full of memories. I don't picture my life in any other country. This is my home, and all I'm asking for is the chance to be able to stay and build my life—without the fear of being deported."[4]

THE PATH TO CITIZENSHIP

Praeli's desire to be a US citizen is one she shares with millions of other people. Between 2005 and 2015, the number of naturalized citizens in the United States increased by 37 percent—from 14.4 million to 19.8 million.[5] Naturalization is the process where people who weren't born in the United States can become US citizens. The highest rates of naturalization are among immigrants from Ecuador, India, Peru, and Haiti.

In 2017, people across the country wanted to keep the DACA program in place.

To begin the process, immigrants must submit an application to the US Citizenship and Immigration Services (USCIS). Applicants have their fingerprints documented and photographs taken. These are used for background checks. Next, the applicants meet with an immigration officer. At this time, applicants explain their history and take a civics test. The questions test the applicant's knowledge of the United States. One sample question might ask who needs to sign bills in order for them to become law. Those who pass the test then swear an oath of loyalty to the United States, and the immigrant is then officially a legal US citizen.

Applying for naturalization isn't a guarantee of becoming a citizen. Between 2005 and 2015, the federal government denied nearly one million naturalization requests. This number amounts to approximately 11 percent of naturalization applications filed during this time.[6] And the process can be slow—especially since the number of applications has been surging. The time can range from ten months to

Washington, Immigrants, and Citizens

George Washington understood the importance of immigration and citizenship in building the United States. "I had always hoped that this land might become a safe & agreeable Asylum to the virtuous & persecuted part of mankind, to whatever nation they might belong," Washington wrote in 1788. He envisioned the new nation as one where people might "settle themselves in comfort, freedom and ease in some corner of the vast regions of America."[7]

Taking the Test

The US citizenship test has two parts. One part is an English test. It tests the applicant's ability to speak, read, and write in English. An immigration officer asks the applicant to read and write sentences in English, as well as answer basic questions. Another part is the civics test. It evaluates the applicant's knowledge of US government and history. To pass the civics test, an applicant must correctly answer six of ten questions.

26 months, depending on the area where a person lives and how many people are applying there. Added to this are steep fees. As of 2019, the fee to file for naturalization was more than $600.[8]

THE DREAM OF CITIZENSHIP

Being a legal US citizen comes with many rights. These rights are outlined in the US Constitution. In theory, these rights apply to anyone on US soil. But in practice, the rights are often denied to people who aren't citizens. For example, the Constitution guarantees fast, fair trials by a jury. But in 2013, approximately 83 percent of people who were deported didn't receive any kind of hearing or trial.[9]

Civil rights are just the beginning of benefits for US citizens. For instance, citizens can travel abroad using a US passport. This document allows citizens to visit many different countries without visas. Citizens can sponsor family members who would like to immigrate to the United States. And citizens are eligible for government benefits. These include food stamps, federal aid for college, health insurance, and public housing programs.

People who want to travel internationally need passports.

The rights connected to citizenship haven't always been within reach for all people. Throughout history, attitudes about race have determined who could become a citizen. At first, only free white people could be citizens. This requirement kept citizenship out of reach for the nation's large population of enslaved Africans. Later, new laws prevented Chinese immigrants from citizenship solely based upon their race. And during

Reasons for Naturalization

There are many reasons a person might want to become a US citizen. Jutka Emoke Barabas became a citizen in 2000 after fleeing Hungary. "For me, American citizenship means freedom of expression and to live and work in a free country . . . and not [having] to be afraid of being arrested or harassed because of owning certain common books or pictures. To be an American is not just a great honor, but also an obligation to do more and reach higher," she said.[10]

Stephen Park is from Scotland and became a citizen in 2005. He said this about citizenship: "No other country gives you the right to pursue happiness, and that is the right that I have grabbed firmly with both hands. A lot of people complain about this country . . . but try living elsewhere without all the rights that you take for granted. In some ways, we immigrants are the lucky ones; we see more clearly the opportunities that this great nation affords all its people."[11]

Valeria Richards views different people coming together in the United States as a good thing. "When I arrived in the US from Italy I went back to school and started working as a registered nurse in a hospital. I became a citizen after holding a permanent green card for 32 years . . . I was proud to be in a room full of every possible race and ethnicity. I was part of what makes America great: its diversity and its acceptance of anyone who comes here with dreams and good intentions," she said.[12]

World War II (1939–1945), Japanese Americans temporarily lost citizenship rights.

Throughout history, countless leaders have fought to make citizenship available to people regardless of race. Today, that tradition continues on with advocates such as Praeli. She serves in the role of government relations manager at an organization called Forward, a bipartisan political group. Forward is attempting to reform immigration laws and the criminal justice system. In doing so, the goal is to ensure all people in the United States have a fair chance at reaching their full potential.

In this role, Praeli represents Dreamers. Her voice joins with thousands of advocates who have fought barriers to citizenship throughout the nation's history. "My hope is for Congress to act with urgency to pass narrow, targeted legislation that will permanently protect Dreamers like me," said Praeli. "Our great nation is deserving of the many contributions that Dreamers like me provide. We have built a life full of memories in the United States and are just asking for the chance to continue to build those in the country we call home."[13]

DISCUSSION STARTERS

- Dreamers were brought into the United States as minors. They were too young to make the decision to enter the United States on their own. What do you think the government should do about Dreamers in the United States?
- The process of naturalization can take years to complete. Why do you think immigrants choose to go through the process? Do you think there are any negative aspects to becoming a US citizen?

CHAPTER TWO

CITIZENSHIP AND WHITENESS

Delegates met in Philadelphia, Pennsylvania, in the summer of 1787. Their task was to draft a document to create their new nation's government. The result was the US Constitution. This document spells out how the government works. It also guarantees specific rights to people on its soil.

Many of the rights in the US Constitution apply to anyone living within the borders of the United States. But some are reserved for citizens only, such as the right to vote in a federal election. Today, if undocumented immigrants vote in a federal election, they could face up to three years in prison and deportation. The Constitution also protects people against unreasonable searches and seizures. This means if law enforcement officers suspect a person of committing a crime,

The US Constitution helped lay the framework for the government of the United States. However, it didn't give every person in the country equal rights.

We the People of the United States, in Order to form a more pe
insure domestic Tranquility, provide for the common defence, promote the general Welfare, and secure the Bl
and our Posterity, do ordain and establish this Constitution for the United States of America.

Article. I.

Section. 1. All legislative Powers herein granted shall be vested in a Congress of the United States, which shall
of Representatives.

Section. 2. The House of Representatives shall be composed of Members chosen every second Year by the People o
in each State shall have the Qualifications requisite for Electors of the most numerous Branch of the State Legislature.

No Person shall be a Representative who shall not have attained to the Age of twenty five Years, and been seven
and who shall not, when elected, be an Inhabitant of that State in which he shall be chosen.

Representatives and direct Taxes shall be apportioned among the several States which may be included within this U
Numbers, which shall be determined by adding to the whole Number of free Persons, including those bound to Service for a T
not taxed, three fifths of all other Persons. The actual Enumeration shall be made within three Years after the first Meeti
and within every subsequent Term of ten Years, in such Manner as they shall by Law direct. The Number of Represen
thirty Thousand, but each State shall have at Least one Representative; and until such enumeration shall be made, the S
entitled to chuse three, Massachusetts eight, Rhode Island and Providence Plantations one, Connecticut five, New York
eight, Delaware one, Maryland six, Virginia ten, North Carolina five, South Carolina five, and Georgia three.

When vacancies happen in the Representation from any State, the Executive Authority thereof shall issue Writs of

The House of Representatives shall chuse their Speaker and other Officers; and shall have the sole Power of Impe

Section. 3. The Senate of the United States shall be composed of two Senators from each State, chosen by the Legislatu
Senator shall have one Vote.

Immediately after they shall be assembled in Consequence of the first Election, they shall be divided as equally a
of the Senators of the first Class shall be vacated at the Expiration of the second Year, of the second Class at the Expiration
Class at the Expiration of the sixth Year, so that one third may be chosen every second Year; and if Vacancies happen by R
Recess of the Legislature of any State, the Executive thereof may make temporary Appointments until the next Meeting of the
such Vacancies.

No Person shall be a Senator who shall not have attained to the Age of thirty Years, and been nine Years a Citizen
not, when elected, be an Inhabitant of that State for which he shall be chosen.

The Vice President of the United States shall be President of the Senate, but shall have no Vote, unless they be equally d

The Senate shall chuse their other Officers, and also a President pro tempore, in the Absence of the Vice President, or w
President of the United States.

The Senate shall have the sole Power to try all Impeachments. When sitting for that Purpose, they shall be on O
of the United States is tried, the Chief Justice shall preside: And no Person shall be convicted without the Concurrence of two thirds o

Judgment in Cases of Impeachment shall not extend further than to removal from Office, and disqualification to
Trust or Profit under the United States: but the Party convicted shall nevertheless be liable and subject to Indictment, Tr
according to Law.

Section. 4. The Times, Places and Manner of holding Elections for Senators and Representatives, shall be prescrib
thereof; but the Congress may at any time by Law make or alter such Regulations, except as to the Places of chusing Senato

The Congress shall assemble at least once in every Year, and such Meeting shall be on the first Monday in D
appoint a different Day.

Section. 5. Each House shall be the Judge of the Elections, Returns and Qualifications of its own Members, and a M
Quorum to do Business; but a smaller Number may adjourn from day to day, and may be authorized to compel the A
such Manner, and under such Penalties as each House may provide.

Each House may determine the Rules of its Proceedings, punish its Members for disorderly Behaviour, and, with t
Member.

Each House shall keep a Journal of its Proceedings, and from time to time publish the same, excepting such Par
Secrecy; and the Yeas and Nays of the Members of either House on any question shall at the Desire of one fifth of those Presen

Neither House, during the Session of Congress, shall, without the Consent of the other, adjourn for more than th
than that in which the two Houses shall be sitting.

Section. 6. The Senators and Representatives shall receive a Compensation for their Services, to be ascertained by
the United States. They shall in all Cases, except Treason, Felony and Breach of the Peace, be privileged from Arrest
Session of their respective Houses, and in going to and returning from the same; and for any Speech or Debate in either H
any other Place.

No Senator or Representative shall, during the Time for which he was elected, be appointed to any civil Office un
which shall have been created, or the Emoluments whereof shall have been encreased during such time; and no Person h
States, shall be a Member of either House during his Continuance in Office.

Section. 7. All Bills for raising Revenue shall originate in the House of Representatives; but the Senate may propose or

Every Bill which shall have passed the House of Representatives and the Senate, shall, before it become a Law, be

Voting fraud does not happen often in US elections.

they can't search his or her property for evidence of the crime without permission from a judge. For undocumented immigrants who cross the border, this right doesn't apply. Search and seizure for anyone who crosses the border is considered by some people as reasonable, and it is allowed.

Despite its many details, the Constitution doesn't specify one key idea. It doesn't determine who can and can't become a citizen. This was done intentionally. The framers of the Constitution wanted to leave that decision in the hands of lawmakers. And as a result, determining who qualifies for citizenship has shifted over time with the nation's changing views on race, politics, and religion.

In March 1790, Congress passed the Naturalization Act, the nation's first law regarding citizenship. It specified who was eligible for citizenship. The law stated that free, white immigrants who lived in the United States for at least two years could apply for citizenship.

LEGAL UNCERTAINTY

Legal status for nonwhite people living in the United States was complex in the nation's early history. In the South, slavery was legal. Enslaved people weren't considered citizens, even if they had been born in the United States and lived there for their whole lives. In the North, the situation was different. There, slavery was illegal and most nonwhite people were free. Despite being free, they weren't always recognized as citizens. African American communities began to push for the abolition of slavery and equal treatment under the law.

One of the most influential African American communities was in Baltimore, Maryland.

Excluded Populations

The Naturalization Act of 1790 had a far-reaching impact for people living in the United States. It disqualified entire populations of the country who weren't free or white from becoming citizens. According to the US Census, the nation had a population of almost 3.9 million in 1790. The Naturalization Act excluded nearly 20 percent of that population from citizenship because they were nonwhite, enslaved people.[1] The law also disqualified indentured servants, free African Americans, Native Americans, and Asians from citizenship.

Maryland was a free state, and the African Americans in Baltimore pushed for birthright citizenship. They argued that anyone born in the United States was a citizen, regardless of skin color or status as free or enslaved. They also fought to end slavery. They

In the 2010s, Baltimore was a majority-black community.

used churches, newspapers, and courtrooms as platforms to get their message to the public.

Other leaders of the time pushed for a different solution. They believed the best course of action was for free African Americans to deport themselves, known as self-deportation. A number of white citizens agreed with that idea. African Americans appeared to have two choices. They could leave the United States and start over elsewhere. Or, they could stay and attempt to create a life in a nation where their status was uncertain.

Many chose to stay and attempted to solve the problems of freedom and citizenship. One of the most well known of these people was Dred Scott. Scott was an enslaved person who found himself in the middle of a legal battle that went to the Supreme Court. The outcome not only affected Scott but also influenced the role of African Americans and citizenship for the next several decades.

THE DRED SCOTT DECISION

Dred Scott lived in Missouri, where slavery was legal. Scott's slaveholder was John Emerson. Emerson worked for the US Army as a surgeon. In 1834, Emerson's job required him to travel, and he took Scott with him. The army stationed Emerson in Illinois. It was a state where slavery was illegal. Emerson also traveled to Wisconsin, which was a territory that didn't allow slavery.

Dred Scott went with John Emerson to different places in the United States where slavery was illegal.

Scott joined Emerson in both places. Then the men returned to Missouri.

Emerson died in 1843. After Emerson's death, Scott tried to purchase his freedom. But Emerson's wife, Irene, refused the request. With the help of antislavery lawyers, Scott and his wife, Harriet, sued Irene. In 1847, he took the case to court. Scott's argument was that because he and Emerson had lived in a free state and a free territory, Scott had been emancipated. The case was known as *Scott v. Emerson*. It went through the court system for ten years and had a series of judgments and appeals.

In 1850, Irene moved out of Missouri. She turned over possession of her estate, including ownership of Scott, to her brother John Sanford. Sanford, whose last name was misspelled by the court, continued to appeal the case. *Scott v. Sandford* headed to the US Supreme Court in 1857. The court's decision would be final. It couldn't be appealed to another court. Chief Justice Roger Brooke Taney wrote the court's opinion, which explains how the justices reached their decision. In *Scott v. Sandford*, Taney wrote that under the US Constitution, Scott wasn't a citizen. Because of this, he had no rights under the law to sue someone in a federal court.

In the opinion, Taney outlined under what circumstances a free person of color could legally receive citizenship. He noted that states could make their own law that bestowed citizenship upon free people of color. However, this citizenship would only be valid in the state that issued it. Therefore, a free person of color could never have federal citizenship. So even if Scott had received citizenship in Missouri, he couldn't have sued Sanford in the federal courts.

CHANGES AFTER THE CIVIL WAR

The *Scott v. Sandford* decision sent ripples of emotion throughout the nation. Americans were already deeply divided between those who favored slavery and those who opposed it. The

North was antislavery, and many Northerners were outraged by the court's decision. People who lived in the South, which was in favor of slavery, saw the decision as a victory. The divisions between the North and South continued to grow in the years after the case. The division ultimately led to the Civil War (1861–1865).

The war ended when the South surrendered on April 9, 1865. The following years were dedicated to rebuilding the nation. The states ratified the Thirteenth Amendment to the Constitution on December 6, 1865. It officially made slavery illegal in the United States. It stated, "Neither slavery nor involuntary servitude, except as a punishment for crime whereof the party shall have been duly convicted, shall exist within the United States, or any place subject to their jurisdiction."[2]

The outlawing of slavery was a huge victory for free and enslaved blacks. But the issue of citizenship for the recently freed slaves remained unclear. While they were now free, they were still disqualified from citizenship because they weren't white.

The Scotts Finally Win Freedom

Scott and Harriet ultimately did receive their freedom. Irene Emerson's second husband, Calvin Chaffee, was a well-known abolitionist. He learned that the man at the heart of the Scott case was part of his wife's estate. At that time, a husband could control his wife's property. Chaffee immediately arranged for Scott's emancipation. Around two months after the Supreme Court decision, the Scotts were formally freed at the Saint Louis Circuit Court.

In an attempt to repair this fact, Congress passed the Civil Rights Act of 1866. It stated that anyone born in the United States was automatically a citizen. This meant that any recently freed slaves were now legal US citizens.

The Civil Rights Act could be repealed or changed. So some lawmakers looked for a more permanent solution. The result was the first clause in the Fourteenth Amendment to the US Constitution. This amendment was ratified on July 28, 1868. The amendment states, "All persons born or naturalized in the United States, and subject to the jurisdiction thereof, are citizens of the United States and of the state wherein they reside."[3] It also prevented any states from stripping citizens of this protection.

Birthright vs. Blood

The two main ways people across the globe receive their citizenship are through *jus soli* or *jus sanguinis*. In Latin, the term *jus soli* means "right of the soil." It is the legal term that is commonly referred to as birthright citizenship. Under this law, a person becomes a citizen of the nation in which he or she was born. It is what the Civil Rights Act of 1866 made into a federal law. In developed countries, this is the most common way of becoming a citizen, and it's the method used in the United States and Canada.

In other places, citizenship is determined by *jus sanguinis*, which means "right of blood" in Latin. Under this system, children inherit their citizenship from their parents. This system is common in European countries. So, if a child has a mother from a *jus sanguinis* country, a father from a different *jus sanguinis* country, and the child is born in a *jus soli* country, that child could have citizenship in three different countries.

In 2018, President Donald Trump talked about ending birthright citizenship as outlined in the Fourteenth Amendment. However, as of mid-2019, no action had been taken to do so.

To make the issue even clearer, Congress revised its Naturalization Act in 1870. It changed the language in the act to specifically include people of African descent. While the struggles for African Americans weren't over, they had cleared a major hurdle. At long last, they had won the battle to be US citizens.

While this was a victory, it wasn't the end of the story of racism and citizenship. People of other races soon found themselves up against similar racist laws. In just a matter of years, Chinese immigrants would be facing a similar battle.

DISCUSSION STARTERS

- The framers of the US Constitution intentionally chose to not include the requirements for citizenship. Why do you think they did this? Do you agree with their decision? Why or why not?
- Dred Scott pushed against the common ideas of how an enslaved person could gain freedom. What effect did his actions have on the idea of citizenship and race? Did his case hurt or help other enslaved people in winning their freedom and citizenship?
- Why did Congress decide to include birthright citizenship as part of the Fourteenth Amendment to the US Constitution? Do you think the framers of the Constitution would have agreed with the amendment? Why or why not?

EXCLUDING THE CHINESE

For the first several decades of US history, most immigrants came from Europe or Africa. Few came from Asia. That changed in 1840 when China opened its borders. For the first time in history, its subjects had the freedom to leave China and travel to other places. During this time, the United States became interested in trading with China. It was a brand-new market for US goods.

As US trade ships traveled to China, they brought news with them. One of the most exciting stories was the discovery of gold in California in 1848. At that time in China, floods, famines, and poverty were taking a toll on the people. The idea of leaving these problems behind and striking it rich in California led to the first mass migrations of Chinese people to the United States.

Starting in the late 1840s, tens of thousands of Chinese people came to the United States in search of gold.

At first, all appeared to go well. But problems started to arise as an increasing number of gold miners worked the land. The white miners grew angry and mistrustful of the Chinese miners. The Chinese language, clothing, and food were much different from their own. The Chinese miners also looked different. These dissimilarities made some white miners view their Chinese counterparts as strangers who didn't belong in California.

Chinese immigrants had another option for work in 1862, when the US government began building the transcontinental railroad. It would connect the East and West Coasts of the country for the first time. The Central Pacific Railroad started in California and worked eastward. The Union Pacific Railroad started on the Iowa-Nebraska border, where existing railroads

The Central Pacific Railroad hired many Chinese immigrants to lay tracks across the Sierra Nevada.

ended, and worked westward. The two railroads planned to meet in the middle.

The majority of the Central Pacific laborers were Chinese immigrants. They were working on the largest engineering project in the nation at that time. The work was dangerous and difficult. Workers blasted through mountains to build tunnels and laid thousands of miles of railway track. The transcontinental railroad was completed in May 1869. It allowed people to travel from one coast to the other much more quickly and comfortably than before. It allowed goods to be shipped easily. And it also encouraged Americans to develop new cities and towns in the West.

Racist Rhetoric

When the transcontinental railroad was completed, thousands of Chinese laborers lost their jobs. The large pool of cheap labor scared many US workers. People continued to treat Chinese immigrants badly. This racist column from February 6, 1869, appeared in *Workingman's Advocate* magazine just months before the railroad's completion. It illustrates the negative attitudes people had toward Chinese workers in the country:

> *We warn workingmen that a new and dangerous foe looms up in the far west. . . . Men [from China] who can work for a dollar a day are a dangerous element in our country. We must not sleep until the foe is upon us, but commence to fight him now. In the name of the workingmen of our common country, we demand that our government forbid another [Chinese person] to set foot upon our shores.*[1]

Chinese laborers made a major contribution to the railroad's construction and the

Chinese immigrants established communities throughout the United States. Some communities today, such as in New York City, are called Chinatowns.

nation's development. Despite this, they continued to face violence and hatred. In 1873, a depression hit the US economy. Jobs became difficult to find. Some Americans didn't like competing with Chinese laborers to find work. They feared the

Chinese immigrants were taking jobs away from white workers. They demanded that Congress take action. The result was a history-making law rooted in racism.

THE CHINESE EXCLUSION ACT AND ITS EFFECT

In the spring of 1882, US Congress passed the Immigration Act. It later became known as the Chinese Exclusion Act. This law had a far-reaching impact on Chinese immigration. The official reason for the law was stated as, "The coming of Chinese laborers to this country endangers the good order of certain localities within the territory."[2] Many Chinese immigrants believed the true reason for passing the law was racism.

The Chinese Exclusion Act was the first federal law to stop immigration based solely upon a person's nationality. The act suspended immigration of any skilled or unskilled laborers from China for a period of ten years. The only Chinese people allowed to enter the United States were those who planned to stay for a short time, such as tourists or students. Any ship's captain who violated these terms by transporting Chinese laborers faced steep fines and jail time.

The act also had a far-reaching impact on Chinese immigrants already living in the United States. It blocked any Chinese immigrants from becoming naturalized citizens. And the act created new restrictions on traveling. If Chinese immigrants chose to travel outside the United States, they needed a special government-issued identification certificate. Upon return to the United States, any immigrant without the certificate would be turned away.

The effect of the act was swift. In 1882, an estimated 39,000 Chinese immigrants entered the country. The next year, that number had dropped to 8,031. By 1884, only 279 Chinese people entered the United States.[3] Due to the hostile feelings in California, many Chinese immigrants moved east. They built new businesses and homes in cities such as Boston, New York City, and Chicago.

FIGHTING BACK

As time passed, members of the Chinese American community began to fight back against the act. They wrote letters and editorials in newspapers blasting the government for its actions. They also sued the government. Between 1882 and 1905, Chinese immigrants filed more than 10,000 lawsuits in federal courts. Approximately 20 of the cases wound up in the US Supreme Court.[4]

One of the most noteworthy cases to reach the Supreme Court was known as *United States v. Wong Kim Ark*. At the heart of the case was the issue of citizenship. The Chinese Exclusion Act forbade the

The Six Companies

The Six Companies was a collection of community groups that supported Chinese immigrants. If immigrants faced problems with debt, the groups helped settle them. The Six Companies maintained registries of immigrants and acted as a link between workers and employers. If immigrants faced legal troubles, the groups also provided aid.

Wong Kim Ark's case was monumental in cementing the concept of birthright citizenship.

government from naturalizing any Chinese immigrant. However, that wasn't the only law at play in this case. The Fourteenth Amendment to the Constitution also applied. It stated that anyone born in the United States was a citizen.

Wong Kim Ark found himself in a tug-of-war between these two federal laws. Wong had been born in San Francisco, California, to parents who were Chinese immigrants. They were technically still subjects of the Chinese emperor, since they couldn't become naturalized US citizens. But they lived and worked in San Francisco. It was the only home Wong had ever known.

Wong's parents moved back to China in 1890. He traveled there to visit them several times. Upon one return trip, Wong met a collector of customs named John Wise. Wise's anti-Chinese sentiments were well known. He wanted to make an example out of Wong, and he denied Wong reentry into the United States. Wise claimed that Wong couldn't be a US citizen because his parents weren't US citizens. Wong argued that he had been born on US soil and was therefore a citizen by birth. Wise refused to let Wong off the ship, where Wong stayed for several months while getting legal help.

UNITED STATES V. WONG KIM ARK

Wong's case began in the district court of Northern California. In 1897, the US Supreme Court heard Wong's case. The US Justice

Department claimed that Wong couldn't become a citizen merely "by the accident of birth."[5] Because Wong's parents weren't—and, at the time, couldn't become—US citizens, neither could Wong. In contrast, Wong's lawyers leaned heavily on the Fourteenth Amendment and its language on birthright citizenship.

The case captured the nation's attention. Immigrants across the country waited for the outcome. If Wong wasn't allowed to be considered a citizen, they wondered whether their own children would face similar battles. In March 1898, the court made a decision. To the surprise of many Americans, it sided in Wong's favor. Being born in the United States did, indeed, automatically make Wong a citizen—regardless of the statuses of his parents. It was a major victory against the racist policies that attempted to keep citizenship from Chinese immigrants.

The Great Fire

A devastating earthquake hit San Francisco in 1906. It killed around 3,000 people, destroyed 500 city blocks, and left one-half of the city's residents homeless.[6] It also triggered what became known as the Great Fire. The fire destroyed many buildings, including those that held immigration records. "Dating from the Great Fire, many, many, Chinese became 'born in the United States,' and there was no means to disprove the claims because the records had been completely destroyed," said author Betty Lee Sung in her book *The Story of the Chinese in America*. "That is not to say that all such claims were false, but to separate the wheat from the chaff was difficult and a native-born citizen was not to be denied his constitutional rights."[7]

Wong's victory set the precedent for birthright citizenship cases. It is still cited in court cases today. Despite the case's outcome, little changed for Chinese immigrants. The Chinese Exclusion Act had been intended to last only ten years, but Congress renewed it several times. Each renewal continued to block any immigration from China. It would take another 60 years and numerous laws to reverse the suspension of Chinese immigration and naturalization.

DISCUSSION STARTERS

- Should the US government have aided the unemployed Chinese laborers after the transcontinental railroad was complete? Why or why not?
- The Chinese Exclusion Act was the first federal law to deny immigration and citizenship based upon nationality. Do you think another law like this could ever be passed in the United States? Why or why not?

CHAPTER FOUR

AN INCREASE IN IMMIGRANTS

Since its dedication in 1886, the Statue of Liberty has towered over New York Harbor. It is one of the nation's best-known symbols of immigration. The torch in the statue's upraised hand serves as a gesture of welcome. Engraved on the statue's base is a poem by Emma Lazarus. Its final lines state, "Give me your tired, your poor, [y]our huddled masses yearning to breathe free, The wretched refuse of your teeming shore. Send these, the homeless, tempest-tost to me, I lift my lamp beside the golden door!"[1]

The Statue of Liberty was one of the first sights many immigrants saw when they arrived in the United States. Ships glided past the statue on their way to Ellis Island, home of the largest and busiest immigration station in the nation. Agents

Many people see the Statue of Liberty as a symbol welcoming immigrants to the United States.

there processed more than 12 million immigrants between 1892 and 1924.[2] During these years, the United States had an open-door policy on immigration, with the exception of the Chinese Exclusion Act. Under this policy, the US government placed no restrictions on the number of immigrants allowed into the country.

Not all Americans agreed with the open-door policy. Over time, these feelings led to a movement known as nativism.

Saum Song Bo

The Chinese Exclusion Act prevented immigrant Saum Song Bo from becoming a citizen. When he received a request to help fund a pedestal for the Statue of Liberty, he wrote a letter to the *New York Sun* in June 1885 expressing the irony of that request in the face of the Chinese Exclusion Act.

> *A paper was presented to me yesterday for subscription among my countrymen toward the Pedestal Fund of the Statue of Liberty. My countrymen and myself are honored in being thus appealed to as citizens in the cause of liberty. But the word liberty makes me think of the fact that this country is the land of liberty for men of all nations except the Chinese. That statue represents Liberty holding a torch—which lights the passage of those of all nations who come into this country. But are the Chinese allowed to come? Are the Chinese here allowed to enjoy liberty as men of all other nationalities enjoy it? Free from the insults, abuse, assaults, wrongs and injuries from which men of other nationalities are free? By the law of this nation, a [Chinese person] cannot become a citizen. Whether this statute against the Chinese—or the Statue of Liberty—will be the more lasting monument to tell future ages of the liberty and greatness of this country, will be known only to future generations.*[3]

Nativists wanted to protect the interests of native-born citizens over those of immigrants. Around this time, immigration patterns also began to change. Unrest in southern and eastern Europe created a surge of people from this area coming to the United States. Some Americans considered these immigrants less desirable than those who came from western Europe. The growing popularity of this line of thinking led to a new attitude toward US immigration based upon race.

NATIVISM SPREADS

People who agreed with nativist thinking believed that for the United States to prosper, it needed a solid base of English citizens. One of the outspoken leaders of this group was a scientist named Nathaniel S. Shaler. At first Shaler argued against the newcomers based on class. Most were poor and uneducated. He later shifted this idea from class to race. He believed immigrants from southern and eastern Europe were so racially different that they couldn't become Americanized.

Shaler wasn't alone. His ideas were supported by Massachusetts senator Henry Cabot Lodge. Lodge undertook a survey on immigration in 1891. He concluded that the "English racial strain" had provided more to the development of the United States than any other group.[4] He also suggested that without controlling immigration, Americans' national character would be "bred out."[5]

At Angel Island Immigration Station in California, officials gave physical examinations to some immigrants.

CHANGES IN 1907

In an attempt to reform immigration policy, Congress passed an act on February 20, 1907. It doubled the tax for immigrants entering the United States from $2 to $4.[6] In 2019 terms, that money would be an increase from around $54 to $108.[7] Many of the immigrants from southern and eastern Europe were poor. This tax increase made immigration more difficult for them. It was a thinly veiled attempt to keep them out of the country.

The 1907 act also placed specific restrictions on physical and mental conditions that had not existed earlier. The act harshly stated that "all . . . feeble-minded persons, epileptics, and insane persons" were denied access.[8] Likewise, anyone considered a beggar or impoverished person couldn't enter the country. Anyone suffering from a contagious disease, such as tuberculosis, was also not allowed to enter. If an immigrant's ticket had been paid for by a business that planned to employ the immigrant as a laborer, the immigrant was also denied access on the grounds of taking jobs from Americans. People who violated these laws would be sent back to their home countries.

Four days after this act passed, President Theodore Roosevelt made an agreement with Japan that also affected immigration. Racial tensions had been escalating in California. The state had seen a large wave of Japanese immigrants. History professor Roger Daniels explained this tension by saying, "The anti-Japanese movement was in many ways merely a continuation of the long-standing agitation against the Chinese."[9]

Some San Francisco citizens organized a Japanese and Korean Exclusion League. Its members threatened to force all Asian children to attend segregated schools. Japan was upset

The Dillingham Commission was named after its chairperson, Vermont senator William P. Dillingham.

with this proposal. As tensions grew, President Roosevelt decided to step in. He worked directly with Japan's leaders. In 1907, they came to an understanding known as the Gentleman's Agreement. Japan agreed to stop issuing passports to laborers. It also acknowledged the right of the US government to deny entry to Japanese citizens. In return, the people pushing for Asian exclusion in San Francisco schools withdrew their request for segregation.

"Not Bona Fide Citizens"

Anti-Japanese feelings had grown hostile in San Francisco. On May 7, 1900, labor leaders held an anti-Japanese protest. The city's mayor, James Duval Phelan, expressed the common feelings about Japanese Americans at the time. His words were harsh: "The Japanese are starting the same tide of immigration which we thought we had checked twenty years ago. . . . The Chinese and Japanese are not bona fide citizens. They are not the stuff of which American citizens can be made. . . . Personally we have nothing against Japanese, but as they will not assimilate with us and their social life is so different from ours, let them keep at a respectful distance."[10]

DILLINGHAM COMMISSION

In 1907, Congress commissioned an in-depth study in an attempt to get more information on past and present US immigration. It became known as the Dillingham Commission. The commission's goal was to reach a compromise. Lawmakers hoped its findings would help them create policies to bridge the gap between nativists

and those who supported open-door immigration. In 1911, the Dillingham Commission released its findings and made policy recommendations.

One of the commission's members, William Husband, recommended a quota plan based upon the 1910 census. The census included data about the population of different racial groups. Immigrants of each race would be limited to 5 percent of the existing population of that group in the United States. At the time, race often meant the same thing as nationality or ethnicity. For example, the number of immigrants from Italy couldn't exceed 5 percent of the total number of Italians already living in the United States. In this way, the quota system could keep those populations small and prevent a flood of people from immigrating to the county.

The commission also recommended a literacy test. If immigrants couldn't read or write—either in English or their native language—they couldn't enter the United States. The idea behind this recommendation was to make sure the new citizens were educated. Literacy test opponents argued that reading and writing had more to do with opportunity than intelligence. If an immigrant couldn't read, it didn't mean she or he wasn't intelligent. It just meant the immigrant hadn't had the chance to attend school. This was the case for many immigrants from southern and eastern Europe.

WORLD WAR I AND ITS AFTERMATH

Before lawmakers could put the Dillingham Commission's recommendations in place, the United States faced a new danger. World War I (1914–1918) began in Europe in 1914. It involved nearly all the nations on that continent. On one side were the Central powers. They included Germany, Austria-Hungary, and Turkey. On the other side were the Allies, which included Britain, France, and Russia. In 1917, the United States joined the Allies in fighting the Central powers.

German Americans

German Americans encountered mistrust and dislike during World War I. According to the 1910 US Census, the German population in the United States totaled eight million. Of that number, around 2.5 million were born in Germany.[11] The rest were native-born citizens.

When the United States entered the war, German Americans fell under suspicion. People accused them of being German spies. At that time, a hyphen was often used between *German* and *American*. They became known as hyphenated Americans. It referred to the idea that immigrants might still have some allegiance to Germany. Some Americans believed that if the immigrants were truly loyal to the United States, they would stop identifying as German. President Woodrow Wilson went so far as to say, "Any man who carries a hyphen about with him, carries a dagger that he is ready to plunge into the vitals of this Republic when he gets ready."[12]

The results of these anti-German feelings led the government to create four incarceration camps. Many German immigrants had legal paperwork. They were living in the United States peacefully, working to meet the residency requirements to become naturalized citizens. But because of their ethnicity, they were removed from their homes and sent to live in the camps until the war's end.

When the war started, immigration slowed to a trickle. Immigrating was too dangerous and difficult during wartime. But the strong ideas of nativism still existed in the United States. A fierce sense of patriotism, stirred up by the American involvement in the war, also grew across the nation. The result was strong feelings of xenophobia—fear, mistrust, and dislike of foreigners.

The uncertainty and fear created by the war gave rise to strict new immigration laws. As World War I raged in Europe, Congress moved forward with new laws aimed at curbing immigration based on ethnicity and race. The Immigration Act of 1917 maintained the physical and mental guidelines established in the 1907 act. In addition, immigrants were required to pass the literacy test that the Dillingham Commission had recommended before the war. Any immigrant age 16 or older had to read a passage of text. Immigrants didn't have to read in English, however. They could choose the language for the reading test. The new restrictions meant that in 1917, immigration

East Indian Immigrants

In the early 1900s, some Indian immigrants came to California to work in agriculture. Just like the Chinese and Japanese, they faced racism in the United States. Indian immigrants were also affected by anti-Asian legislation in 1917, as India was included in the Asiatic Barred Zone.

services turned away 16,028 immigrants—4.2 percent—for not meeting the new guidelines.[13]

The Immigration Act of 1917 also targeted immigrants from specific countries. The Chinese Exclusion Act remained in effect, banning immigrants from China. But the 1917 act went even further. It extended the ban to include people from other parts of Asia as well. This area became known as the Asiatic Barred Zone. It included eastern Asia and the Pacific Islands. One exception existed, however. Filipinos were allowed to immigrate because the Philippines was a US colony.

DISCUSSION STARTERS

- Do you think nativism still exists today? Why or why not?
- In what ways did Americans of this era connect race, social class, and ethnicity? Why do you think those three factors were important to them? Do you think those factors play any role in people's views about immigration today?
- How do you think the quota system affected US society? Do you think it still affects US society today? Why or why not?

NATIVE AMERICAN CITIZENSHIP

For many years, the status of Native Americans as US citizens remained largely unsettled. Most Native Americans weren't considered citizens. They weren't eligible to be naturalized, either.

During World War I, an estimated 9,000 Native Americans served in the US armed forces.[14] However, most weren't US citizens. They placed their lives in danger for a country that didn't provide them with basic rights. When the war ended, Congress passed the American Indian Citizenship Act of 1919. It allowed Native American veterans to apply for US citizenship.

Five years later, Congress created another citizenship law. On June 2, 1924, President Calvin Coolidge signed the Indian Citizenship Act. It granted US citizenship to all Native Americans born in the United States. The US government didn't pass the law because of pressure from Native American groups to make them citizens. Instead, the government passed the law in an attempt to assimilate Native Americans into US society.

Despite the law, Native Americans didn't receive all their rights. They still faced racism in many areas. Many Native Americans faced obstacles such as poll taxes and Jim Crow laws, similar to what African Americans faced. Until 1948, Native Americans weren't allowed to vote in Arizona or New Mexico. These actions became illegal when Congress passed the Civil Rights Act of 1964. It outlawed discrimination based on race, color, religion, sex, or national origin.

President Calvin Coolidge, *center*, met with members of the Osage Nation after the Indian Citizenship Act was passed.

CHAPTER FIVE

EUGENICS, LAWS, AND WAR

World War I ended in 1918. The war's effects were far-reaching. The US public had grown increasingly isolationist. Citizens wanted to stay out of other nations' affairs. They also wanted to keep immigration rates low. At this time, an idea called eugenics became popular. It proposed that the future of a society could be improved by passing down specific genetic traits. It relied on the idea that some races had traits that were superior to others. By eliminating undesirable traits, eugenicists believed the human race could be advanced. Today, eugenics has been dismissed as a false science that proposed dangerous ideas. At this period in history, however, many people believed it had the potential to improve society.

Francis Galton was born in 1822. He coined the term *eugenics* and believed that selective breeding was a way to better humanity.

In 1920, Congress asked eugenics expert Harry Laughlin to testify about immigration. Laughlin stated, "The character of a nation is determined primarily by its racial qualities."[1] Laughlin and many other eugenics supporters believed immigrants from southern and eastern Europe would bring undesirable genetic traits with them. Eugenicists began to refer to immigrants unfairly as "inferior stock" and "unfit" citizens.[2] They feared the immigrants might dilute the purity of Americans. As a result, the United States might become a weaker nation.

A False Idea of a Superior Race

One of the leaders in the anti-immigration movement was New York lawyer Madison Grant. In 1916, he wrote a book about eugenics called *The Passing of the Great Race*. It influenced many people's attitudes about race. "To admit the unchangeable differentiation of race in its modern scientific meaning is to admit inevitably the existence of superiority in one race and of inferiority in another," wrote Grant. "The Anglo-Saxon branch of the Nordic race is again showing itself to be that upon which the nation must chiefly depend for leadership, for courage, for loyalty, for unity and harmony of action."[3]

While these ideas gained popularity in the United States, immigration increased. The war's end had made immigration safer and easier. Many southern and eastern Europeans wanted to escape the war's destruction. Once again, immigration rates began to rise. Some Americans didn't want to compete with immigrants for limited resources, such as jobs and land. And they were suspicious of the immigrants' backgrounds. They spoke unfamiliar languages such as Italian and Russian. And many immigrants were Catholic or Jewish. These religions weren't common among the largely Protestant nation.

With these factors in play, this period saw an increased push for stronger immigration reforms. On May 24, 1924, President Coolidge signed the strictest immigration law in US history. It was known by two names: the Johnson-Reed Act and the National Origins Act. It created a quota system. The quotas were much stricter than what the Dillingham Commission had recommended before World War I.

Coolidge's Address

President Calvin Coolidge took office in 1923. That year, he gave his first State of the Union speech to Congress. In it, he directly addressed the growing concerns about immigration and the future of the United States. "American institutions rest solely on good citizenship," said Coolidge. "They were created by people who had a background of self-government. New arrivals should be limited to our capacity to absorb them into the ranks of good citizenship. America must be kept American."[5]

THE NATIONAL ORIGINS ACT

Under the National Origins Act, Congress created quotas. The total number of immigrants allowed to enter the United States each year was 150,000.[4] The quotas were based upon the 1890 census. Newer census data was available, but lawmakers ignored it. They chose to use the 1890 census because it contained a larger percentage of northern Europeans. This in turn affected the quotas. Each nation received a quota of 2 percent of the number of people of the same national origin in 1890.[6] Wording the law this way favored certain immigrants from northern and western Europe.

The Asiatic Barred Zone remained in effect under the National Origins Act. It still forbade people from the zone from immigrating. People from China were also still excluded from immigration, as the Chinese Exclusion Act had been renewed several times. And the 1907 agreement where Japan voluntarily limited the rate of immigration still remained in place.

The National Origins Act slowed immigration. But two other factors had a major impact. The first was the Great Depression. This economic downturn started in the United States in 1929,

Mexican Deportation

During the 1930s, finding jobs became increasingly difficult, and people began to blame people of Mexican descent. White citizens accused them of taking jobs that didn't belong to them. Anyone with a Mexican last name fell under suspicion. For this reason, more than one million people of Mexican descent were forced to return to Mexico in the 1930s. Sixty percent of them were legal US citizens—many of them had been born in the United States.[7] Many of the children forced to leave had never been to Mexico and didn't speak Spanish fluently. They found themselves in a foreign country without any documents to prove their US citizenship. The deportations weren't part of any formal federal plan. Instead, they were carried out by local governments and businesses in cities such as Chicago, Illinois; Los Angeles, California; and Detroit, Michigan.

and it quickly spread to many countries throughout the world. It lasted approximately ten years. During this time, millions of people were out of work. The second factor was the start of World War II in 1939. Just as in World War I, immigration became too costly and dangerous.

EXECUTIVE ORDER 9066

As World War II began in Europe, the United States pledged to stay out of the conflict. But on December 7, 1941, Japanese pilots bombed a fleet of navy ships docked at Pearl Harbor, Hawaii. The attack killed 2,403 people and injured thousands of others.[8] The next day, Congress declared war on Japan. Three days later, Japan's ally Germany declared war on the United States.

At the time of the attack, an estimated 125,000 people of Japanese heritage lived in the United States. Another 200,000 lived in Hawaii, which was a US territory at the time.[9] Some employees at the US War Department became suspicious of Japanese Americans. They worried that the Japanese Americans might be spies, which they believed would compromise the nation's security. No evidence supported this theory, but that didn't stop the government from taking actions against its own citizens of Japanese heritage.

On February 19, 1942, President Franklin Roosevelt signed Executive Order 9066. It authorized the US military to organize a mass evacuation of Japanese Americans. A month later, Congress passed a bill authorizing the military to use force to relocate

After the attack on Pearl Harbor, a Japanese American business owner put a sign in front of his business in Oakland, California.

Japanese Americans as part of the war effort. They had to leave behind their jobs, homes, furniture, toys, and even pets. They could only take items that they could carry. The property they left behind was often stolen or vandalized.

Within six months, more than 122,000 men, women, and children of Japanese ancestry had been forced into incarceration camps. Approximately 70,000 people of Japanese descent were US citizens.[10] They had been convicted of no crimes, but they were being treated as criminals solely because of their race.

INCARCERATION CAMPS

The government set up ten incarceration camps for Japanese Americans. The camps had schools, farmland, work facilities, and post offices. Despite this, the living conditions were crowded barracks that had been built quickly. An average barrack was 20 feet (6 m) by 100 feet (30 m), and it housed between four and six families. Each block in a camp typically had 14 barracks, which housed approximately 300 people.[11] In these close quarters, diseases such as smallpox and typhoid spread quickly. The barracks were freezing in the winters and blazing hot in the summers. The barracks had no plumbing, and people had to use bathrooms, showers, and laundry facilities located elsewhere in the camp. The incarceration camps were surrounded by barbed wire and armed guards to prevent escape.

Mary Tsukamoto and her family lived in an incarceration camp in Jerome, Arkansas. She later recalled what it was like to enter the camp and face a new reality. "We saw all these people behind the fence, looking out,

Japanese American Soldiers

After Pearl Harbor, Japanese American men of a certain age were no longer allowed to serve in the military, although this decision was eventually reversed in early 1943. Many Japanese Americans in the military acted as translators. They deciphered data such as maps and battle plans and intercepted messages. Around 33,000 Japanese Americans served in the US military during the war.[12] Mark Murakami, a Japanese American soldier in the war, spoke about the contradictions of this service: "[On] the one hand the Japanese Americans were condemned for having the linguistic and cultural knowledge of Japanese. And on the other hand the knowledge they had was capitalized on and used as a secret weapon by the Army and Naval Intelligence."[13]

Japanese Americans were targets of racism. They were forced into incarceration camps during World War II.

hanging onto the wire, and looking out because they were anxious to know who was coming in. But I will never forget the shocking feeling that human beings were behind this fence like animals [crying]. And we were going to also lose our freedom and walk inside of that gate and find ourselves . . . cooped up there. . . . When the gates were shut, we knew that we had lost something that was very precious; that we were no longer free."[14]

The incarceration camps operated throughout the war. When the war ended in 1945, people were slowly freed from the camps. The last one closed in March 1946. Today, this forced internment is considered one of the worst civil rights violations in US history. At the time, Japanese Americans had few options to fight it. Some people took cases to the court system to challenge the order. But ultimately, the US Supreme Court held that Executive Order 9066 was legal and constitutional.

DISCUSSION STARTERS

- Do you think countries should have rules about who can live within their borders?
- How might people's privilege play into their fear, or lack of fear, of losing their citizenship?

CHAPTER SIX

AN ERA OF REFORM

When World War II ended in 1945, it ushered in an era of immigration reforms. Congress passed a series of new laws that began the slow process of removing race as a barrier to immigration and naturalization. Lawmakers also began rethinking the use of quotas, which favored certain nationalities.

During these years, the biggest influence on immigration was the Cold War. This rivalry between the United States and the Soviet Union didn't involve direct military warfare. Each country had a different type of government. The United States was democratic. The Soviet Union was communist. But they both wanted world power. The rivalry created mistrust, threats, and fear.

After World War II, the United States allowed Jewish refugees into the country. But it had denied asylum to thousands of Jewish refugees during the war.

The only nuclear bombs used in wartime were dropped on Japan by the United States.

Concerns over the Cold War influenced immigration reforms and who was allowed to enter the country. Some Americans worried the Soviet Union would drop a nuclear bomb on the United States. Others became suspicious of immigrants from eastern Europe, which had close ties to the Soviet Union. Lawmakers worried immigrants from this area would infiltrate the government and spread communism. These fears created a renewed desire to understand who was entering the United States and what their influence might be.

THE McCARRAN-WALTER ACT

In 1947, Congress authorized a committee to complete a long-term study on immigration. Four years later, the committee members reported their findings. They discovered that an estimated 60 percent of all immigrants worldwide chose to come to the United States. Canada was the next most popular destination. An estimated 11.5 percent of all immigrants moved to Canada. The remaining 28.5 percent of immigrants chose to move to Argentina, Brazil, Australia, New Zealand, and South Africa.[1]

The committee also revealed that immigration was a patchwork of laws, executive orders, enactments, treaties, regulations, and rules. Each one related to a different aspect of US immigration and naturalization. The committee recommended streamlining all of them into one act. Senator

Pat McCarran and Representative Francis Walter undertook that job. The result was the McCarran-Walter Act.

Under the proposed act, the quota system would remain in place. It was a way to prevent more immigrants from arriving than the nation could support. As in the past, the quotas mirrored the national origins of the existing US population. Of the 154,277 visas available, more than 85 percent went to people from northern Europe.[2] Applicants with job skills or family members in the United States also received preference under the quotas.

The new act also attempted to remove race as a barrier to immigration and naturalization. Every nation—even those that had been banned earlier—now received a minimum quota of 100 people per year.[3] This meant people from China, Japan, and other parts of Asia were able to immigrate and become legal citizens for the first time in decades.

According to McCarran, the quotas remained low for Asian nations because assimilation

Symbolic Changes

Critics saw the changes in the McCarran-Walter Act as symbolic only. The number of visas Asian nations received was small compared to those of other nations. And the Asian immigrant quotas were still based on race rather than nationality. For example, if an immigrant were born and raised in the United Kingdom but had Chinese parents, that immigrant would count against China's quota rather than the United Kingdom's.

would be harder for people from Asia. He and others believed this slow assimilation could weaken the nation. "I believe that this nation is the last hope of western civilization," said McCarran when reflecting on the act. He added, "I take no issue with those who would praise the contributions which have been made to our society by people of many races. . . . However, we have in the United States today hard-core indigestible blocs who have not become integrated into the American way of life but which, on the contrary, are its deadly enemies."[4]

In April 1952, Congress passed the McCarran-Walter Act. When it reached the desk of President Harry S. Truman, he vetoed it. Truman believed it was discriminatory and that its purpose was to "cut down and virtually eliminate immigration to this country from Southern and Eastern Europe. . . . The idea behind this discriminatory policy was, to put it baldly, that Americans with English or Irish names were better people and better citizens than Americans with Italian or Greek or Polish names. . . . This quota system keeps out the very people we want to bring in." Truman went further, saying that quotas were "utterly unworthy of our traditions and our ideals. It violates the great political doctrine of the Declaration of Independence that 'all men are created equal.'"[5] Despite Truman's efforts, Congress overruled his veto. The act went into effect in December 1952 and would remain in effect until the mid-1960s.

The Hart-Celler Act is also known as the Immigration and Nationality Act of 1965. President Lyndon B. Johnson signed it at the foot of the Statue of Liberty.

THE HART-CELLER ACT

In the 1950s and 1960s, the civil rights movement swept through the United States. Its supporters sought to end segregation and ensure all races had equal rights. Civil rights leaders held peaceful protests and marches to draw attention to their cause. In 1964,

Congress passed the Civil Rights Act. The law made it illegal for anyone to practice "discrimination or segregation on the ground of race, color, religion, or national origin."[6]

In this era of social change, ideas about citizenship and immigration also began to change. "We have removed all

President Johnson spoke to reporters about the Hart-Celler Act.

elements of second-class citizenship from our laws by the [1964] Civil Rights Act," said Vice President Hubert Humphrey. "We must in 1965 remove all elements in our immigration law which suggest there are second-class people."[7] Later that year, President Lyndon B. Johnson signed a sweeping new immigration law, the Hart-Celler Act.

The Hart-Celler Act ended the quota systems that had been in place since the 1920s. A person's country of origin no longer stood as a barrier to immigration. The Hart-Celler Act created caps to replace quotas. The cap was the highest number of immigrants that could be allowed per year. The act set a cap of 170,000 immigrants from the Eastern Hemisphere per year. This included Asia, as well as most of Africa and Europe. The Western Hemisphere received a yearly cap of 120,000 immigrants. This

Speaking Against the Quota System

The Hart-Celler Act disbanded the quota system when it came to immigration. This system was one main reason President Harry S. Truman disagreed with the McCarran-Walter Act. When he spoke to Congress about the McCarran-Walter Act in 1952 he said:

> *Today, we are "protecting" ourselves, as we were in 1924, against being flooded by immigrants from Eastern Europe. . . . The countries of Eastern Europe have fallen under the communist yoke—they are silenced, fenced off by barbed wire and minefields—no one passes their borders but at the risk of his life. We do not need to be protected against immigrants from these countries—on the contrary we want to stretch out a helping hand, to save those who have managed to flee into Western Europe . . . to welcome and restore them against the day when their countries will, as we hope, be free again.*[8]

included North and South America.[9]

To determine who could make up the people in the caps, the Hart-Celler Act used a preference scale. It favored spouses and children of US residents. They would be eligible for 74 percent of all visas. Twenty percent of the visas would go to professionals, scientists, artists, and laborers. The remaining 6 percent of visas would be set aside for refugees.[10]

Changing Demographics

The Hart-Celler Act of 1965 changed the makeup of immigrants entering the United States. Before the act, more than one-half of all immigrants came from Europe. That changed quickly after the act passed. Between 1965 and 2000, the largest number of immigrants came from Mexico. During the same period, large numbers of immigrants arrived from the Philippines, Korea, the Dominican Republic, India, Cuba, and Vietnam.

The preference system still gave the government full control over who entered the nation. But the goal of the preference system was to serve the interests of US businesses and residents. "The bill establishes a new system of selection [of immigrants] designed to be fair, rational, humane, and in the national interest," said Senator Ted Kennedy, one of the act's supporters.[11]

The preference system set up in the Hart-Celler Act guided US immigration for decades. Over time, the government made a few amendments to the act. In 1976, Congress limited each country to 20,000 visas per year. It had the biggest impact on

Mexico, which was the only country actively seeking more than 20,000 visas on a regular basis. Two years later, Congress eliminated the caps based upon hemisphere. It issued 290,000 visas total, regardless of hemisphere.[12]

DISCUSSION STARTERS

- Do you think it is fair for immigration policies to favor skilled workers over immigrants who might be viewed as unskilled? Explain your answer.
- President Truman vetoed the McCarran-Walter Act because he thought it was discriminatory. Do you agree? Why do you think Congress overrode the veto?
- The 1960s were a decade of changes in US civil rights. It was also a time of great changes for immigration. The Hart-Celler Act of 1965 removed quotas for the first time in more than 40 years. How do the two changes reflect similar trends in society?

NEW CHALLENGES

By the late 1970s, a growing number of refugees began to dominate the discussion about immigration and citizenship. At the time, many of the refugees were from Vietnam. Communists in North Vietnam were fighting with South Vietnam and its allies, including the United States. But in April 1975, communists succeeded in taking over Vietnam. It led to a flood of refugees from Indochina, a region that included Vietnam, Laos, and Cambodia.

These refugees looked to the United States for help. Around 130,000 people from Vietnam, Cambodia, and Laos came to the United States in 1975 alone.[1] By 1979, the situation had grown more dire. President Jimmy Carter doubled the number of these refugees allowed into the United States to 14,000 each month.[2]

Some Vietnamese refugees were able to live with family members who were US citizens.

3921

Not all Americans welcomed the refugees, however. A month after Carter's increase, a poll showed that more than 62 percent of Americans disapproved of the increase in refugees.[3]

In light of the enormous demand for refugee help, Congress took action in 1980. That year it passed the Federal Refugee Resettlement Program. This program screens refugees and determines who is admitted to the United States. The program's goal is to help refugees resettle and adapt to life in a new country. Between 1980 and 1990, around 590,000 refugees from Indochina settled in the United States.[4]

It wasn't often an easy transition into a new country. Some Americans made it even more difficult by taking advantage of the refugees. Hoang Chi Truong was 13 years old when her family fled Vietnam and moved to the United States. "It was the dawn of a new day—on so many levels," recalled Truong. "I remember wanting to kiss the ground. To be in a free land." But life soon took a difficult

Early Refugees

The United States passed its first law regarding refugees in 1948. That year, it allowed 250,000 Europeans who had been displaced by World War II to immigrate. This number didn't count against the national origin quotas. The United States later expanded this number to allow 400,000 European refugees to enter the country.[5] Later, the United States expanded this further to accept refugees who were leaving communist countries. They included places such as Hungary, Poland, Yugoslavia, Korea, China, and Cuba.

turn when they received jobs at a lodge in Wyoming. They lived in a cramped crawl space, cooking and cleaning for no wages. "All I can say is we were being exploited, taken advantage of and oppressed," Truong said.[6]

THE "THREE-LEGGED STOOL"

In addition to refugees, immigration without permission from the US government became another pressing issue in the 1980s. Many undocumented immigrants feared being discovered by the government, which could lead to deportation. For this reason, they didn't report their presence in the United States to the government. As a result, the government didn't have any official figures of how many undocumented people were in the country. However, the US Census Bureau estimated that in 1986, between three and five million undocumented immigrants lived in the United

Shifting the Viewpoint

Some Americans fear that immigrants are taking away good jobs from US citizens. Others argue that immigrants receive more from the government than they contribute. In truth, this is not the case. Immigrants pay more in taxes than they receive in government benefits. And many industries rely on immigrants to thrive. In the agriculture industry, for example, many of the sales and financial jobs go to native-born Americans. But they couldn't do their jobs without the immigrants who work on the farms. The immigrants and the native-born workers complement each other. Neither could survive without the other. And as US birth rates drop and people retire, immigrants are filling jobs that would otherwise remain vacant.

States.[7] Some experts believed the number was actually much higher.

Many of the undocumented immigrants came from Mexico in search of jobs. Lawmakers believed that the promise of jobs was fueling unauthorized immigration. They thought that if they made getting jobs more difficult, this immigration would slow down. So Congress passed the Immigration and Reform Control Act of 1986 (IRCA). It was the most sweeping immigration law in many years. And it had three major parts. For this reason, some

In the late 1900s, the majority of farmworkers were immigrants.

of the lawmakers who wrote the act called it the "three-legged stool."[8] They believed each leg was an important part of reducing unauthorized immigration.

The IRCA's first leg involved security. It created stronger penalties for using forged identity documents, such as passports. Anyone who knowingly transported or harbored undocumented people also faced more serious penalties than in the past. The IRCA increased the number of border patrols. And it also gave greater power to the Immigration and Naturalization Service (INS). This agency was responsible for enforcing immigration laws.

The second leg of the IRCA stool focused on employers. Any employer who knowingly hired undocumented immigrants faced federal civil and criminal penalties. It was the first time this had ever happened. The act also created the I-9 process. It was a program for employers to verify and document the legal status of anyone they hired. The act took measures to prevent documented immigrants from facing discrimination. It forbids an employer to discriminate based on an applicant's national origin or legal status.

The third leg of the stool addressed those undocumented immigrants who were already in the United States. The IRCA created a pathway to citizenship for them. Rather than hiding, unauthorized immigrants were encouraged to come forward to the government. It would provide them amnesty. Their illegal arrival would be overlooked. Anyone who had been living in the United States as of January 1, 1982, or earlier could apply for legal resident status. If they met the residency requirements and passed the civics test, they could then become naturalized citizens.

President Ronald Reagan signed the bill into law on November 6, 1986. Before he signed it, he commented that it was "the most comprehensive reform of our immigration laws since 1952."[9] He and the lawmakers who wrote the bill believed it would provide a fair way to improve the borders as well as the lives of undocumented immigrants. Reagan said, "Future generations of Americans will be thankful for our efforts to humanely regain control of our borders and thereby preserve the value

Family Migration

The IRCA granted amnesty to millions of undocumented immigrants. Amnesty is the act of pardoning the immigrants who hadn't followed the proper legal path to enter the United States. In the years following the amnesty, many Americans became concerned about a practice known as family migration. It happens when the family member of a US citizen applies for a visa. Family members receive preference over other immigrants who don't have families living in the United States.

Through 2017, family visas made up 37 percent of all immigrant visas issued for the year.[11] Critics say this can lead to unchecked growth. People can enter the country based largely on whom they are related to. President Donald Trump and others want to change this. They would prefer to use a merit-based system. It would give preference to people with professional training, education, and English skills.

of one of the most sacred possessions of our people: American citizenship."[10]

THE EFFECTS OF 9/11

Views of immigration and citizenship shifted once again after September 11, 2001—also known as 9/11. That morning, members of a Muslim extremist group called al-Qaeda hijacked four US airplanes. Some hijackers flew two planes into the World Trade Center towers in New York City. Others flew a plane into the Pentagon in Virginia. A fourth airplane crashed into a field in Pennsylvania. Nearly 3,000 people died in the attacks.[12] It was the deadliest terrorist attack on US soil.

The terrorists were all foreigners who had entered the United States legally. As a result, the US government became stricter about who could enter the country. Screenings at airports became more thorough. Security at US borders became tighter. And because the terrorists were members of al-Qaeda, the government focused its attention on extremists and the countries that aided them. The United States issued fewer immigration visas in Muslim-majority countries such as Pakistan, Egypt, and Morocco. In addition, between 2001 and 2010, the rate of deportation increased drastically for all immigrants.

One of the most controversial security programs implemented after 9/11 was called the National Security Entry-Exit Registration System (NSEERS). It was a registry with special requirements, such as providing fingerprints,

The World Trade Center towers were destroyed during the 9/11 terrorist attacks.

photographs, and yearly check-ins. However, the registry requirements didn't apply equally to all immigrants. They only applied to those who came from countries singled out by the US government. Most of these countries were in Africa and the Middle East and were predominately Muslim. The tracking only applied to males older than age 16 from those countries.

Entry wasn't the only struggle Muslims faced after 9/11. The process of becoming naturalized citizens grew more difficult. After 9/11, people with Muslim names were subjected to an extra background check before being cleared for citizenship. In many cases, this created lengthy delays for Muslim immigrants. Between 2006 and 2007 alone, more than 93,000 applications for naturalization were delayed because of the extra checks. In many of these cases, the delays ranged from around three to 33 months.[13]

LIFE FOR MUSLIM CITIZENS

For Muslims living in the United States, life changed after 9/11, too. Tasnia Ahamed was nine years old at the time of the attacks. "[Before 9/11] I never felt that anyone ever hated me or my family for being Muslim. Instead, people just weren't familiar with what being Muslim meant. After 9/11, things were definitely different," she said.[14] Muslim Americans reported people yelling racial slurs at them. Some Muslim women chose not to wear a hijab, a traditional head covering, for fear it would attract unwanted attention. In airports, Muslim people discovered that they were pulled aside for extra security screening.

Tahra Goraya was a 28-year-old Muslim woman living in California at the time of the 9/11 attacks. Shortly afterward, she was driving her car and stopped at an intersection when "a couple crossing the street in front of me stopped, pointed at me and started to yell profanities and yelled for me to 'go home,'" said Goraya. "I was shocked, dumfounded, speechless and angry. I wanted to yell back that I was home; this is home." This hostile atmosphere affected people's lives. "My mom . . . was harassed grocery shopping and driving days after the attacks," said Goraya. "She stopped going out altogether and didn't leave the house. My siblings, my dad and I all tried to convince her to

Racial and Ethnic Profiling

Many Muslim Americans have experienced racial or ethnic profiling in the years since 9/11. The American Civil Liberties Union (ACLU) defines profiling as a "discriminatory practice by law enforcement officials of targeting individuals for suspicion of crime based on the individual's race, ethnicity, religion or national origin."[17] For many Muslim American citizens, this is especially noticeable when flying, due to increased security measures at US airports.

"More often than not, almost every single time I'm traveling, I get stopped and I get patted down," said Negeen Sadeghi-Movahed, a Muslim American law student. When she passes through security, she said the agents don't ask her where she's from. Instead, they ask her where her name is from. It's a subtle difference, but one that's not lost on Sadeghi-Movahed. "So I can't go, 'California, born and raised,'" she said. "I have to say my name is Iranian, and it doesn't usually end in my favor." She's also become used to being pulled aside for additional inspections as part of a process called Secondary Security Screening Selection. "It's supposedly random, but the only people I know who've ended up on it are Muslim and usually Iranian," she said.[18]

live her life and not give up on her daily activities like shopping, going to the gym or visiting friends, but she would not have it."[15]

Eighty-two percent of Muslims living in the United States are legal citizens. Of that number, approximately one-half of them were born in the United States. The other half are immigrants who have become naturalized.[16] "There's a great deal of apprehension in the Muslim community as to the demonization of Islam," said Ibrahim Hooper, a spokesman for the Council on

American-Islamic Relations. "A lot of us feel that our patriotism is always suspect."[19]

Amid this atmosphere, suspicion, fear, and hatred of Muslims grew in many US communities. Before 9/11, Muslims had been one of the least-targeted groups in hate crimes. According to the FBI, hate crimes against Muslims jumped by 1,600 percent between 2001 and 2002.[20] These crimes ranged from destroying Muslim places of worship to physical violence and even murder just because a person practices Islam.

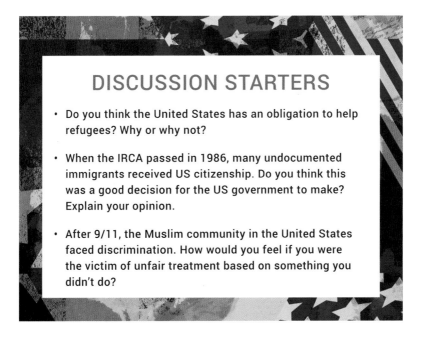

DISCUSSION STARTERS

- Do you think the United States has an obligation to help refugees? Why or why not?
- When the IRCA passed in 1986, many undocumented immigrants received US citizenship. Do you think this was a good decision for the US government to make? Explain your opinion.
- After 9/11, the Muslim community in the United States faced discrimination. How would you feel if you were the victim of unfair treatment based on something you didn't do?

CHAPTER EIGHT

DREAMERS, CARAVANS, AND THE FUTURE

The debate about who can become a citizen is still ongoing. Attitudes about race have changed over the years, but the idea of being careful about choosing new citizens has not. One of the most high-profile and controversial examples of this idea involves the Dreamers.

On June 15, 2012, President Barack Obama spoke to reporters about a group of young people known as Dreamers. In his opening remarks, Obama described the Dreamers as "Americans in their heart, in their minds, in every single way but one: on paper."[1]

The president was encouraging Congress to pass an act to help the Dreamers. He said it made no sense to deport the young people who thought of themselves as Americans and who

President Barack Obama spoke to reporters about DACA in the White House's Rose Garden.

SEAL OF THE PRESIDENT OF THE UNITED STATES

DREAM & PROMISE
#PROTECTTHEDREAM

In 2019, politicians like House of Representatives speaker Nancy Pelosi worked to pass a new DREAM Act.

wanted to contribute to the country. The DREAM Act offered a path to citizenship for these young people. Under the act, if they had lived in the United States for five years and agreed to go to college or serve in the military, they could become US citizens.

Versions of the DREAM Act had been debated in Congress since 2001. But the act never received enough votes to pass. Part of the resistance had to do with border security. An estimated 80 percent of the people who would qualify for this pathway to citizenship came from Mexico.[2] Leaders in Congress argued that they wouldn't pass the bill until the US–Mexico border was more secure. These leaders also believed the act rewarded people for breaking the law and entering the country illegally.

As a result, many of these young people faced an uncertain future. They were no longer children. They needed to pay for college, get driver's licenses, and find jobs. As unauthorized residents, they couldn't do these things. Obama and his administration created a temporary solution. He used his executive power to create the Deferred Action for Childhood Arrivals (DACA) program. DACA would allow Dreamers to get jobs and go to school without fear of deportation.

When Obama spoke about DACA, he acknowledged its shortcomings. It was meant as a way to provide temporary relief until Congress passed a permanent solution. "Now, let's be clear—This is not amnesty, this is not immunity. This is not a path to citizenship. It's not a permanent fix," said Obama. "This is a temporary stopgap measure that lets us focus our resources wisely while giving a degree of relief and hope to talented, driven, patriotic young people. It is the right thing to do."[3] DACA became effective in August 2012.

AN UNCERTAIN FUTURE

When President Trump took office, however, things began to change. On September 5, 2017, Trump announced he wouldn't renew the DACA program. No new applications would be accepted, and current DACA enrollees wouldn't be able to renew their status when it expired. Trump did encourage Congress to pass laws to provide aid to Dreamers. In a tweet on September 14, 2017, Trump referred to wanting to keep the

DACA and Green Cards

DACA doesn't provide a pathway to citizenship. But many DACA enrollees have found ways around this by obtaining a green card. A green card allows a person to live and work permanently in the United States. Not all DACA recipients are eligible for green cards. They must qualify for a program known as advance parole. It is similar to a visa in that it allows an immigrant to leave the United States and then reenter. Reentry creates a loophole. That is because at reentry, the undocumented immigrants under DACA can update their status to legal immigrants. Many critics refer to the loophole as backdoor amnesty. USCIS data shows that tens of thousands of DACA enrollees received their green cards in this manner. Cesar Vargas is one of those people. But for Vargas, the green card is bittersweet, since he still has family members who are undocumented. "Coming out now as 'documented' is disorienting and I don't know how long that will last," said Vargas. "What I am certain of, however, is that no matter my immigration status, I always belonged here. This is my country. This is my home."[4]

Dreamers in the United States by saying, "Does anybody really want to throw out good, educated, and accomplished young people who have jobs, some serving in the military?"[5]

Critics argue that Trump was using this stance as a bargaining chip because all the new acts regarding DACA also required stronger border control measures. Specifically, they would require Congress to support and fund the construction of a massive wall along the US–Mexico border. Building the wall was a campaign promise Trump made while running for president.

Amid the political bickering, as of 2019, future changes regarding DACA were slow to unfold. The Trump administration faced lawsuits over ending the program unlawfully. The suits contended that the Trump administration had violated a federal statute called the Administration Procedure Act when it ended the program. Three federal district courts issued injunctions against the ending of DACA. The injunctions allowed DACA recipients to renew their statuses, even though the program had officially ended. On June 28, 2019, the US Supreme Court agreed to review challenges to the ending of DACA. As of August 2019, DACA's future remained in the hands of the court system.

EXTREME VETTING

DACA wasn't the only immigration issue the Trump administration faced. On January 27, 2017, President Trump issued an executive order barring people from Iraq, Syria, Iran, Sudan, Libya, Somalia, and Yemen from entering the United States for

90 days. These countries are predominately Muslim. The order also stopped refugees from entering for 120 days. Refugees from Syria were blocked from entering the United States indefinitely. Some people refer to the executive order as the Muslim ban.

Many people spoke out against President Donald Trump's travel ban, including Senator Cory Booker of New Jersey.

Trump's order is part of a program he commonly referred to as extreme vetting. *Vetting* is a word describing a careful and critical examination. In this case, the Trump administration wanted to provide a careful and critical examination of people who were allowed into the country. It argued it was a way to make sure dangerous people wouldn't enter the country legally. "We want to ensure that we are not admitting into our country the very threats our soldiers are fighting overseas," said Trump. "We only want to admit those into our country who will support our country, and love deeply our people."[6]

Not all people believed the executive order was in the nation's best interest. Some people believed it was a way to use race and religion to block people from entering the country. The American Civil Liberties Union (ACLU), a nonprofit organization that works to protect people's rights, described the executive order as a "euphemism for discriminating against Muslims."[7] The

The Impact on Refugees

Oxfam America is an organization dedicated to helping people across the globe eliminate injustices caused by poverty. Its president, Raymond Offenheiser, was outspoken about Trump's executive order that closed US borders to refugees and its wider impact. He said the order may provide some measure of safety. But it may also harm some of the world's most defenseless people. "The refugees impacted by today's decision are among the world's most vulnerable people—women, children, and men—who are simply trying to find a safe place to live after fleeing unfathomable violence and loss," said Offenheiser.[8]

Migrant Detention Centers

Under President Donald Trump, the number of migrants who have been detained after trying to illegally cross the US–Mexico border has risen in comparison with Trump's predecessor, President Barack Obama. In 2019, the detention centers were overcrowded. Many Democratic lawmakers said people lived in horrific conditions. Alexandria Ocasio-Cortez is a Democratic member of the House of Representatives from New York. She called the centers "concentration camps" and said when she went to visit, "Officers were keeping women in cells [with] no water & had told them to drink out of the toilets."[11] Republican lawmakers countered this type of criticism by saying that detention centers have always been imperfect. In 2018, around 46,000 migrants were detained.[12]

International Rescue Committee, an agency that provides aid to people in humanitarian crisis, also blasted the order, calling it "harmful and hasty."[9]

MAKING NEW HEADLINES

In fall 2018, another issue regarding citizenship and immigration made headlines. On October 12, 2018, a group of 160 migrants from Honduras decided to seek asylum in the United States. They left their country on foot. Along the route, thousands of other migrants joined them. By the time the group reached the Mexico–Guatemala border, it included more than 7,322 people, according to the United Nations.[10] Most were seeking relief from the poverty, violence, and uncertainty in their countries.

The caravan captured the world's attention. Some Americans thought that the nation's borders would be flooded with undocumented immigrants. Many worried legal US citizens would be responsible for paying for the immigrants' care. By the time the caravan reached the US border, however, many people had splintered off from it. They attempted to travel across the border in smaller groups, rather than in one large mass. Many found themselves stuck in Mexican border towns for months waiting to hear whether their requests for asylum had been granted.

US Census Citizenship Question

Every ten years, people living in the United States participate in a census. When it first started, its goal was simply to count residents. The population counts of each state determined how many representatives they had in the US House of Representatives. Over time, Congress granted the census permission to ask other questions about residents, such as their age, race, and level of education.

In 2019, President Trump requested that a new question be added to the 2020 census to determine who is a citizen. Critics believed the question would prevent noncitizens from filling out the census. This would impact communities because census data is used to distribute federal funds and determine the number of representatives each state is allowed. However, in June 2019, the US Supreme Court blocked the question from being added.

CHANGING IDEAS ABOUT CITIZENSHIP

Who should be granted US citizenship became a hot topic of debate during Trump's

Some people are born with US citizenship, while others have to seek it out.

The Rules of Citizenship

In a 2014 opinion-editorial in the *Los Angeles Times*, lawyer and writer Peter Schuck talked about what it means to be a citizen in the United States in the 2000s. He notes that the rules are changing but that that is just as American as citizenship itself. According to Schuck:

> *To Americans, the rules of citizenship can seem simple: You're a member of this nation either by birth or naturalization. But centuries of debate over how citizenship can be acquired and lost show that the concept is not simple at all. . . . The founders and their descendants avoided the hard political, moral and legal questions about membership posed by Indians, slaves and black freemen. . . . Most Americans, however, seem untroubled by the conflicting principles, tolerating an awkward status quo.*[13]

presidency, but the tension surrounding this issue was anything but new. It has existed since the nation's creation and is closely tied to immigration laws. From the beginning, Americans have debated who qualifies as a citizen. The framers of the US Constitution didn't outline the specifics of what makes a person eligible for citizenship. As a result, the laws regarding citizenship have shifted and changed over the country's history.

Over the years, citizenship has been denied to many groups. Early in US history, racist laws denied citizenship to African Americans and Chinese immigrants. Later, these laws were changed, but the debate about citizenship continued. Japanese Americans, for example, had their rights as US citizens temporarily suspended

Many people work hard to achieve US citizenship.

during World War II. More recently, Trump issued a travel ban on people from seven predominately Muslim countries. Their inability to enter the United States puts the path to US citizenship far out of their reach.

Throughout all of these eras, people denied citizenship have taken it upon themselves to fight for their rights. Amendments to the Constitution, Supreme Court rulings, legislative acts, and executive orders have all opened the door to new groups of US citizens. As the United States continues to evolve and grow, laws about who is allowed to be part of its nation will undoubtedly change, too. It is a debate that continues to draw passion from all sides. The outcome will ultimately decide what it means to be a US citizen.

DISCUSSION STARTERS

- What are the similarities between early citizenship debates and today's debates? Are there solutions from the past that might help create solutions to today's issues?
- The concept of extreme vetting has become a lightning rod in US politics. Do you think this process is ethical? What are some other ways the United States could balance security and immigration?

ESSENTIAL FACTS

SIGNIFICANT EVENTS

- Congress passed the Naturalization Act of 1790. This allowed free white residents to qualify to become naturalized citizens.
- The Supreme Court issued a decision on the case of *Scott v. Sandford* in 1857. It ruled that African Americans can be citizens of a state but are not federal citizens.
- The Fourteenth Amendment was ratified in 1868. It granted citizenship to almost everyone born on US soil.
- Congress passed the Chinese Exclusion Act in 1882. It was the first federal law to stop immigration and naturalization of a group based upon nationality.
- In 1924, Congress passed the strictest immigration regulations in US history. The most striking part of the law was the first-ever quota system based on national origin.
- Congress passed the Indian Citizenship Act in 1924, granting citizenship to all Native Americans for the first time in US history.
- During World War II, many Americans of Japanese descent lost their civil rights as citizens. They were placed into camps based solely upon race, despite no evidence of wrongdoing.
- In 1965, the United States passed a more liberal immigration law known as the Hart-Celler Act. It eliminated quotas and gave preference to families and professionals.
- In the 1970s and 1980s, immigration and citizenship focused on refugees and how to resettle them in the United States.
- After the terrorist attacks of 9/11, US immigration policy changed to adapt to a perceived new threat from Muslim extremists such as al-Qaeda.

KEY PLAYERS

- Dred Scott sued his slaveholder for freedom. His case was brought to the Supreme Court.
- Wong Kim Ark took his citizenship case to the Supreme Court. The court ruled that a person's parents do not need to be citizens for their child to be a citizen, as long as that child was born on US soil.
- Americans Nathaniel S. Shaler, Henry Cabot Lodge, and Harry Laughlin used eugenics as a way to justify racist and classist immigration policies.
- President Harry S. Truman vetoed and openly spoke out against the McCarran-Walter Act of 1952, which included immigration policies that Truman considered discriminatory.
- President Barack Obama issued an executive order known as DACA, which gave Dreamers the opportunity to legally work and go to school in the United States without the threat of deportation.
- President Donald Trump refused to renew DACA unless Congress passed stronger measures to protect the US–Mexico border.

IMPACT ON SOCIETY

The United States has always been a nation of immigrants, but which immigrants are allowed to have citizenship has changed over time. Wars, scientific ideas, the economy, and practices such as slavery have all shaped policies about who can become a US citizen. The people whom the US government allows to immigrate and become citizens will shape the future of the nation for generations to come.

QUOTE

"I've grown up in this country, pledged allegiance to our flag since kindergarten, gone to school, and built a life full of memories. I don't picture my life in any other country. This is my home, and all I'm asking for is the chance to be able to stay and build my life—without the fear of being deported."

—Maria Praeli, a Dreamer

GLOSSARY

appeal
A request for a higher court to review the decision of a lower court.

bipartisan
Involving cooperation between the two major political parties.

collector of customs
A historical job held by a federal employee who checks people and goods as they enter a nation.

deport
To force someone to leave a country.

emancipated
Set free.

infiltrate
To gain access to a place or organization gradually in order to obtain secret information.

isolationist
A person who believes his or her country should avoid international conflicts.

naturalize
To become a citizen of a country through immigration rather than birth.

precedent
In court cases, a ruling on a case that serves as a guide for future related rulings.

quota
A fixed quantity of people, money, or things.

ratified
To have formally approved or adopted an idea or document.

vandalized
To have purposefully destroyed or damaged property.

visa
An official authorization permitting entry into and travel within a country.

ADDITIONAL RESOURCES

SELECTED BIBLIOGRAPHY

Gjelten, Tom. "The Immigration Act That Inadvertently Changed America." *Atlantic*, 2 Oct. 2015, theatlantic.com. Accessed 13 June 2019.

Gonzalez-Barrera, Ana, and Jens Manuel Krogstad. "Naturalization Rate among U.S. Immigrants Up since 2015, with India among the Biggest Gainers." *Pew Research Center*, 18 Jan. 2018, pewresearch.org. Accessed 13 June 2019.

Schuck, Peter. "The Complicated Rules of Citizenship." *Los Angeles Times*, 21 Nov. 2014, latimes.com. Accessed 13 June 2019.

FURTHER READINGS

Carser, A. R. *US Immigration Policy*. Abdo, 2018.

Harris, Duchess. *The Dreamers and DACA*. Abdo, 2019.

Rowell, Rebecca. *William Williams Documents Ellis Island Immigrants*. Abdo, 2017.

ONLINE RESOURCES

Booklinks
NONFICTION NETWORK
FREE! ONLINE NONFICTION RESOURCES

To learn more about citizenship, race, and the law, please visit **abdobooklinks.com** or scan this QR code. These links are routinely monitored and updated to provide the most current information available.

MORE INFORMATION

For more information on this subject, contact or visit the following organizations:

INTERNATIONAL RESCUE COMMITTEE

122 East Forty-Second St.
New York, NY 10168-1289
212-551-3000

rescue.org

The International Rescue Committee helps people who are experiencing humanitarian hardship.

US CITIZENSHIP AND IMMIGRATION SERVICES (USCIS)

20 Massachusetts Ave. NW
Washington, DC 20529
800-375-5283

uscis.gov

USCIS is a government agency that administers US immigration laws. Its agents process naturalization applications, help immigrants earn their green cards, aid in international adoptions, and provide training on the rights and responsibilities of US citizens.

SOURCE NOTES

CHAPTER 1. THE DREAM OF CITIZENSHIP

1. "Higher Education and Employment Advancement (HED) Committee Hearing." *Connecticut General Assembly*, n.d., cga.ct.gov. Accessed 15 Aug. 2019.

2. Abigail Robertson. "'I've Been Living on an Emotional Roller Coaster': Dreamers in Limbo as DACA Clock Winds Down." *CBN News*, 11 Jan. 2018, cbn.com. Accessed 15 Aug. 2019

3. Gustavo López and Jens Manuel Krogstad. "Key Facts about Unauthorized Immigrants Enrolled in DACA." *Pew Research Center*, 25 Sept. 2017, pewresearch.org. Accessed 15 Aug. 2019.

4. Stuart Anderson. "Dreamer Wants to Be a US Citizen and Live at Peace." *Forbes*, 29 Jan. 2018, forbes.com. Accessed 15 Aug. 2019.

5. Ana Gonzalez-Barrera and Jens Manuel Krogstad. "Naturalization Rate among US Immigrants Up since 2005, with India among the Biggest Gainers." *Pew Research Center*, 18 Jan. 2018, pewresearch.org. Accessed 15 Aug. 2019.

6. Gonzalez-Barrera and Krogstad. "Naturalization Rate among US Immigrants Up since 2005, with India among the Biggest Gainers."

7. "From George Washington to Francis Adrian Van der Kemp, 28 May 1788." *National Archives*, n.d., founders.archives.gov. Accessed 15 Aug. 2019.

8. "N-400, Application for Naturalization." *US Citizenship and Immigration Services*, n.d., uscis.gov. Accessed 15 Aug. 2019.

9. "What's at Stake." *ACLU*, n.d., aclu.org. Accessed 15 Aug. 2019.

10. Rachel Rodriguez. "Naturalized Citizens Explain Why They're American by Choice." *CNN*, 4 July 2012, cnn.com. Accessed 15 Aug. 2019.

11. Rodriguez, "Naturalized Citizens Explain Why They're American by Choice."

12. Rachel Obordo. "The Day I Became an American Citizen: 'Proud, Grateful, and Hopeful.'" *Guardian*, 6 Feb. 2017, theguardian.com. Accessed 15 Aug. 2019.

13. Maria Praeli. "My Life Is Not a Bargaining Chip. Congress, Protect Dreamers Now." *ABC News*, 2 Feb. 2018, abcnews.go.com. Accessed 15 Aug. 2019.

CHAPTER 2. CITIZENSHIP AND WHITENESS

1. "Return of the Whole Number of Persons within the Several Districts of the United States." *US Census Bureau*, n.d., census.gov. Accessed 15 Aug. 2019.

2. "13th Amendment to the US Constitution: Abolition of Slavery (1865)." *Our Documents*, n.d., ourdocuments.gov. Accessed 15 Aug. 2019.

3. "Fourteenth Amendment and Citizenship." *Library of Congress*, 31 July 2015, loc.gov. Accessed 15 Aug. 2019.

CHAPTER 3. EXCLUDING THE CHINESE

1. "The Chinese Exclusion Act." *PBS*, 29 May 2018, pbs.org. Accessed 15 Aug. 2019.

2. "Transcript of Chinese Exclusion Act (1882)." *Our Documents*, n.d., ourdocuments.gov. Accessed 15 Aug. 2019.

3. John Robert Soennichsen. *The Chinese Exclusion Act of 1882*. Greenwood, 2011. 69.

4. "The Chinese Exclusion Act."

5. "United States v. Wong Kim Ark." *Cornell Law School*, n.d., law.cornell.edu. Accessed 15 Aug. 2019.

6. "San Francisco Earthquake, 1906." *National Archives*, n.d., archives.gov. Accessed 15 Aug. 2019.

7. Soennichsen, *The Chinese Exclusion Act of 1882*, 77–90.

CHAPTER 4. AN INCREASE IN IMMIGRANTS

1. "Statue of Liberty." *Encyclopedia Britannica*, 5 Feb. 2019, britannica.com. Accessed 15 Aug. 2019.

2. "Ellis Island: History & Culture." *National Park Service*, 8 May 2018, nps.gov. Accessed 15 Aug. 2019.

3. "The Chinese Exclusion Act." *PBS*, 29 May 2018, pbs.org. Accessed 15 Aug. 2019.

4. John Higham. *Strangers in the Land: Patterns of American Nativism, 1860–1925*. Rutgers UP, 1955. 140–144.

5. Higham, *Strangers in the Land*, 140–144.

6. Robert DeC. Ward. "The New Immigration Act." *JSTOR*, n.d., jstor.org. Accessed 15 Aug. 2019.

7. "The Inflation Calculator." *West Egg*, n.d., westegg.com. Accessed 15 Aug. 2019.

8. "An Act to Regulate the Immigration of Aliens into the United States." *Library of Congress*, 20 Feb. 1907, loc.gov. Accessed 15 Aug. 2019.

9. Maisie Conrat. *Executive Order 9066: The Internment of 110,000 Japanese Americans*. MIT, 1972. 16.

10. Commission on Wartime Relocation and Internment of Civilians. *Personal Justice Denied*. GPO, 1992. 32.

11. Desmond S. King. *The Liberty of Strangers: Making the American Nation*. Oxford UP, 2005.

12. Robert Siegel and Art Silverman. "During World War I, US Government Propaganda Erased German Culture." *NPR*, 7 Apr. 2017, npr.org. Accessed 15 Aug. 2019.

13. Bureau of Immigration. *Annual Report of the Commissioner General of Immigration to the Secretary of Labor*. GPO, 1919. 15–16.

14. "Citizenship for Native Veterans." *Nebraska Studies*, n.d., nebraskastudies.org. Accessed 15 Aug. 2019.

CHAPTER 5. EUGENICS, LAWS, AND WAR

1. Christopher Petrella. "After Trump." *Boston Review*, 22 Nov. 2016, bostonreview.net. Accessed 15 Aug. 2019.

2. "1910s–1920s: Immigration, Defining Whiteness." *NBC News*, 27 May 2008, nbcnews.com. Accessed 15 Aug. 2019.

3. Lorraine Boissoneault. "Literacy Tests and Asian Exclusion Were the Hallmarks of the 1917 Immigration Act." *Smithsonian*, 6 Feb. 2017, smithsonianmag.com. Accessed 15 Aug. 2019.

4. "The Immigration Act of 1924." *US House of Representatives*, n.d., history.house.gov. Accessed 15 Aug. 2019.

5. "First Annual Message to the Congress." *Calvin Coolidge Presidential Foundation*, 6 Dec. 1923, coolidgefoundation.org. Accessed 15 Aug. 2019.

6. "The Immigration Act of 1924 (the Johnson-Reed Act)." *Office of the Historian*, n.d., history.state.gov. Accessed 15 Aug. 2019.

7. Terry Gross. "America's Forgotten History of Mexican-American 'Repatriation.'" *NPR*, 10 Sept. 2015, npr.org. Accessed 15 Aug. 2019.

8. "How Many People Died at Pearl Harbor during the Attack?" *Pearl Harbor Visitors Bureau*, n.d., visitpearlharbor.org. Accessed 15 Aug. 2019.

9. "Japanese American Internment." *Encyclopedia Britannica*, 3 May 2019, britannica.com. Accessed 15 Aug. 2019.

10. "Executive Order 9066: Resulting in the Relocation of Japanese (1942)." *Our Documents*, 19 Feb. 1942, ourdocuments.gov. Accessed 15 Aug. 2019.

11. "Tule Lake Unit." *National Park Service*, n.d., nps.gov. Accessed 15 Aug. 2019.

12. "Fighting for Democracy: Japanese Americans." *PBS*, n.d., pbs.org. Accessed 15 Aug. 2019.

13. *Personal Justice Denied: Report of the Commission on Wartime Relocation and Internment of Civilians*, U of Washington P, 2012. 254.

14. "Daily Life in the Internment Camps." *National Museum of American History*, n.d., amhistory.si.edu. Accessed 15 Aug. 2019.

CHAPTER 6. AN ERA OF REFORM

1. Pat McCarran. "The Background of the McCarran-Walter Act." *Gov Info*, n.d., govinfo.gov. Accessed 15 Aug. 2019.

2. "The Immigration and Nationality Act of 1952 (the McCarran-Walter Act)." *Office of the Historian*, n.d., history.state.gov. Accessed 15 Aug. 2019.

3. Catherine Walker. "Immigration and Nationality Act of 1953." *Medium*, 5 May 2019, medium.com. Accessed 15 Aug. 2019.

4. McCarran, "The Background of the McCarran-Walter Act."

5. "Veto of the Bill to Revise the Laws Relating to Immigration, Naturalization, and Nationality." *Harry S. Truman Library and Museum*, 25 June 1952, trumanlibrary.gov. Accessed 15 Aug. 2019.

6. "An Act." *EEOC*, 2 July 1964, eeoc.gov. Accessed 15 Aug. 2019.

7. Tom Gjelten. "The Immigration Act That Inadvertently Changed America." *Atlantic*, 2 Oct. 2015, theatlantic.com. Accessed 15 Aug. 2019.

8. "Veto of the Bill to Revise the Laws Relating to Immigration, Naturalization, and Nationality."

9. D'Vera Cohn. "How US Immigration Laws and Rules Have Changed through History." *Pew Research Center*, 30 Sept. 2015, pewresearch.org. Accessed 15 Aug. 2019.

10. Deane and David Heller. "Our New Immigration Law." *American Legion Magazine*, Feb. 1966, archive.legion.org. Accessed 15 Aug. 2019.

11. Heller, "Our New Immigration Law."

12. Cohn, "How US Immigration Laws and Rules Have Changed through History."

CHAPTER 7. NEW CHALLENGES

1. Drew Desilver. "US Public Seldom Has Welcomed Refugees into Country." *Pew Research Center*, 19 Nov. 2015, pewresearch.org. Accessed 15 Aug. 2019.

2. Desilver, "US Public Seldom Has Welcomed Refugees into Country."

3. Desilver, "US Public Seldom Has Welcomed Refugees into Country."

4. Desilver, "US Public Seldom Has Welcomed Refugees into Country."

5. "Annual Refugee Arrival Data by Resettlement State and Country of Origin." *Office of Refugee Resettlement*, 23 Apr. 2019, acf.hhs.gov. Accessed 15 Aug. 2019.

6. Jessica Prois and Kimberly Yam. "Asian 'Boat People,' Once Opposed More Than Syrian Refugees Today, Speak Out." *HuffPost*, 20 June 2018, huffpost.com. Accessed 15 Aug. 2019.

7. Robert Pear. "President Signs Landmark Bill on Immigration." *New York Times*, 7 Nov. 1986, nytimes.com. Accessed 15 Aug. 2019.

8. Muzaffar Chishti. "At Its 25th Anniversary, IRCA's Legacy Lives On." *Migration Policy Institute*, 16 Nov. 2011, migrationpolicy.org. Accessed 15 Aug. 2019.

9. Pear, "President Signs Landmark Bill on Immigration."

10. Pear, "President Signs Landmark Bill on Immigration."

11. John Burnett. "Explaining 'Chain Migration.'" *NPR*, 7 Jan. 2018, npr.org. Accessed 15 Aug. 2019.

12. "9/11 Attacks." *History*, 6 Aug. 2019, history.com. Accessed 15 Aug. 2019.

13. *Race and Ethnicity in America: Turning a Blind Eye to Justice.* American Civil Liberties Union, 2007. 111.

14. Lydia O'Connor. "How 9/11 Changed These Muslim Americans' Lives Forever." *HuffPost*, 12 Sept. 2016, huffpost.com. Accessed 15 Aug. 2019.

15. O'Connor, "How 9/11 Changed These Muslim Americans' Lives Forever."

16. "Demographic Portrait of Muslim Americans." *Pew Research Center*, 26 July 2017, pewforum.org. Accessed 15 Aug. 2019.

17. "Racial Profiling: Definition." *ACLU*, n.d., aclu.com. Accessed 15 Aug. 2019.

18. O'Connor, "How 9/11 Changed These Muslim Americans' Lives Forever."

19. O'Connor, "How 9/11 Changed These Muslim Americans' Lives Forever."

20. Curt Anderson. "FBI: Hate Crimes vs. Muslims Rise." *Associated Press*, 25 Nov. 2002, apnews.com. Accessed 15 Aug. 2019.

CHAPTER 8. DREAMERS, CARAVANS, AND THE FUTURE

1. "Remarks by the President on Immigration." *White House*, 15 June 2012, obamawhitehouse.archives.gov. Accessed 15 Aug. 2019.

2. Gustavo López and Jens Manuel Krogstad. "Key Facts about Unauthorized Immigrants Enrolled in DACA." *Pew Research Center*, 25 Sept. 2017, pewresearch.org. Accessed 15 Aug. 2019.

3. "Remarks by the President on Immigration."

4. Cesar Vargas. "Dreamer: The True Cost of Obtaining My Green Card." *Hill*, 5 June 2018, thehill.com. Accessed 15 Aug. 2019.

5. Ed O'Keefe and David Nakamura. "Trump, Top Democrats Agree to Work on Deal to Save 'Dreamers' from Deportation." *Washington Post*, 14 Sept. 2017, washingtonpost.com. Accessed 15 Aug. 2019.

6. Michael D. Shear and Helene Cooper. "Trump Bars Refugees and Citizens of 7 Muslim Countries." *New York Times*, 27 Jan. 2017, nytimes.com. Accessed 15 Aug. 2019.

7. Shear and Cooper, "Trump Bars Refugees and Citizens of 7 Muslim Countries."

8. Shear and Cooper, "Trump Bars Refugees and Citizens of 7 Muslim Countries."

9. "IRC: Decision to Suspend US Refugee Resettlement Is Hasty and Harmful." *International Rescue Committee*, 27 Jan. 2017, rescue.org. Accessed 15 Aug. 2019.

10. Dara Lind. "The Migrant Caravan, Explained," *Vox*, 25 Oct. 2018, vox.com. Accessed 15 Aug. 2019.

11. Jason Lemon. "Are Migrant Detention Centers Worse Under Donald Trump Than Under Barack Obama?" *Newsweek*, 2 July 2019, newsweek.com. Accessed 15 Aug. 2019.

12. Lemon, "Are Migrant Detention Centers Worse Under Donald Trump Than Under Barack Obama?"

13. Peter Schuck. "The Complicated Rules of Citizenship." *Los Angeles Times*, 21 Nov. 2014, latimes.com. Accessed 15 Aug. 2019.

INDEX

ABOUT THE AUTHORS

DUCHESS HARRIS, JD, PHD

Dr. Harris is a professor of American Studies at Macalester College and curator of the Duchess Harris Collection of ABDO books. She is also the coauthor of the titles in the collection, which features popular selections such as *Hidden Human Computers: The Black Women of NASA* and series including News Literacy and Being Female in America.

Before working with ABDO, Dr. Harris authored several other books on the topics of race, culture, and American history. She served as an associate editor for *Litigation News*, the American Bar Association Section of Litigation's quarterly flagship publication, and was the first editor in chief of *Law Raza*, an interactive online journal covering race and the law, published at William Mitchell College of Law. She has earned a PhD in American Studies from the University of Minnesota and a JD from William Mitchell College of Law.

KATE CONLEY

Kate Conley has been writing nonfiction books for children for more than a decade. When she's not writing, Conley spends her time reading, drawing, and solving crossword puzzles. She lives in Minnesota with her husband and two children.